DINOSAURS Today

By
Teri Crawford Jones

MODERN CURRICULUM PRESS
Pearson Learning Group

The following people have contributed to the development of this product:

Art and Design: Stephen Barth, Salita Mehta, Alison O'Brien
Editorial: Leslie Feierstone Barna, Nicole Iorio, Patricia Peters, Jennifer Serra
Inventory: Levon Carter
Marketing: Alison Bruno
Production: Roxanne Knoll

All photography © Pearson Education, Inc. (PEI) unless otherwise specifically noted.

Photographs: Cover: Demetrio Carrasco © DK Images, 4: © D. Van Ravenswaay/Science Photo Library/Photo Researchers, Inc. 8: Carsten Peter/ National Geographic Image Collection. 10-11: © Will & Deni McIntyre/Photo Researchers, Inc. 12: James L. Amos/ Photo Researchers, Inc. 14: Seth Wenig/Reuters/Corbis. 17: © Tom McHugh/Photo Researchers, Inc. 18: Frans Lanting/Minden Pictures. 21: Tom McHugh Photo Researchers, Inc. 22: Colin Keates © DK Images. Illustrations: 7: Dan Trush

Copyright © 2008 by Pearson Education, Inc., publishing as Modern Curriculum Press®, an imprint of Pearson Learning Group, 299 Jefferson Road, Parsippany, NJ 07054. All rights reserved. No part of this book may be reproduced or transmitted in any form or by any means, electronic or mechanical, including photocopying, recording, or by any information storage and retrieval system, without permission in writing from the publisher. For information regarding permission(s), write to Rights and Permissions Department.

QuickReads®, Modern Curriculum Press®, Developmental Reading Assessment®, and the DRA logo are trademarks, in the U.S. and/or in other countries, of Pearson Education, Inc. or its affiliates(s).

Lexile is a U.S. registered trademark of MetaMetrics, Inc. All rights reserved.

ISBN-13: 978-1-4284-0522-6

ISBN-10:   1-4284-0522-4

Printed in the United States of America
1 2 3 4 5 6 7 8 9 10   11 10 09 08 07

Pearson Learning Group

1-800-321-3106
www.pearsonlearning.com

Contents

What Happened to the Dinosaurs? 5

Dinosaurs Outside Your Window 10

Other Animals From Dinosaur Days . . 16

Glossary 24

What Happened to the Dinosaurs?

Millions of years ago, many kinds of dinosaurs lived on Earth. Some ate plants, while others ate meat. Some dinosaurs were small and fast. Some, like Tyrannosaurus rex, were as tall as trees. About 65 million years ago, the dinosaurs died.

Looking for Reasons

Paleontologists looked deep in the ground for reasons why the dinosaurs died. They saw that Earth went through many changes long ago. Sometimes the air was cool. Then it became warm. When Earth changed, many kinds of animals and plants died or changed, too.

Some scientists think that the dinosaurs may have died after a huge meteor hit Earth.

A scientist named Walter Alvarez made a discovery. He found a clay line in stone and soil. Below the line were many tiny fossils. Above the line were no fossils from the time of the dinosaurs. Something had happened to make that line. Alvarez found the same kind of line in other parts of the world.

Walter Alvarez dug up bits of metal. This metal was usually from rocks called **meteors** that fall from space. He also saw bits of glass. Alvarez knew that when meteors fall to Earth, they are very hot. Meteors could have made the soil hot enough to melt and turn into glass. What Walter Alvarez saw made him think that a huge meteor hit Earth millions of years ago.

A rock that could kill dinosaurs on land must have been big. The rock would have left a huge **crater**. Walter Alvarez could not find such a big hole.

Many scientists looked for the crater. At last, they found a place near Mexico. The place is under the water in the Gulf of Mexico. It is shaped like a crater. In the ground around the Gulf of Mexico, the rocks look as if something hit them hard. There is also ash from big fires. The heat from the meteor would have crushed the trees and set them on fire. Dinosaurs and other animals would have been burned, too.

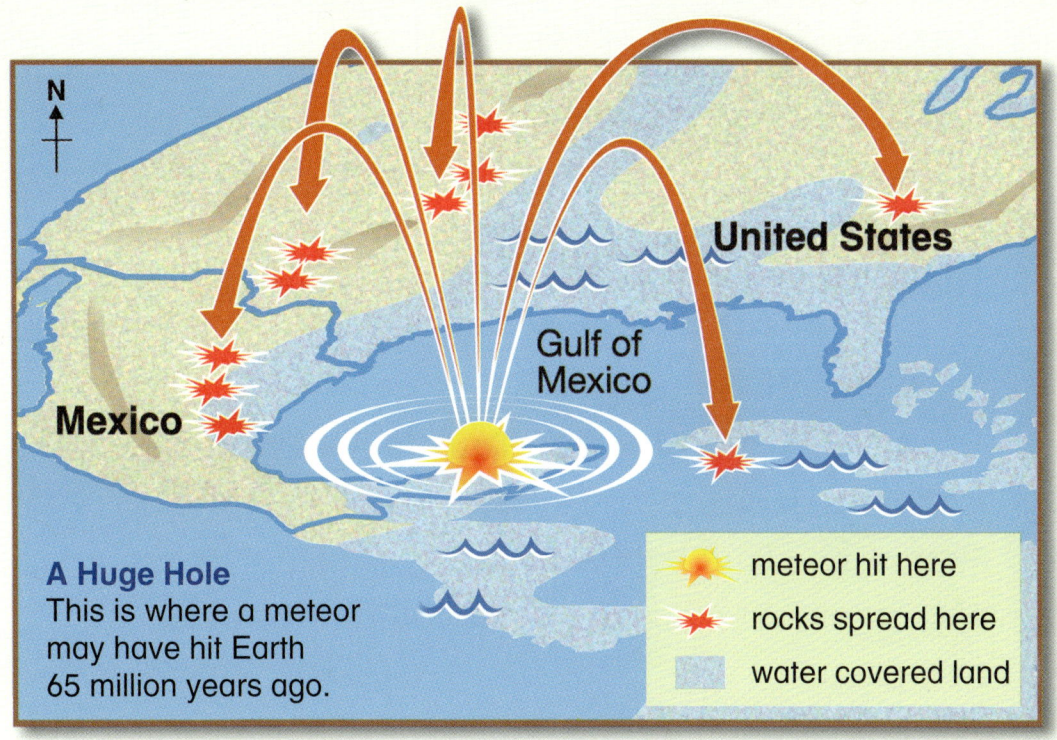

A Huge Hole
This is where a meteor may have hit Earth 65 million years ago.

If fire did not kill the animals, scientists think that huge waves may have. The meteor would have made huge waves when it hit the water. These huge waves would have covered the land with water.

Lots of broken rock and soil must have been tossed into the air when the meteor hit. Dust and dirt may have formed a thick cloud that kept the Sun's light and heat from reaching the ground. The air would be cold. Plants would die. Animals would die because they had no food and could not stay warm.

Volcanoes

Some scientists believe **volcanoes** killed the dinosaurs. The fire from volcanoes would have made clouds of dust just as a meteor would have done. The end was the same. The dinosaurs were gone.

A New Earth

Another reason the dinosaurs may have died is that Earth changed. The oceans began to drain away so the land became dry. Plants died. New plants grew. The big dinosaurs could not eat the new plants.

Many things may have killed the dinosaurs. No one knows for sure. Scientists do know that 65 million years ago the age of the dinosaurs ended.

Dino Notes
Paleontologists have named about 700 kinds of dinosaurs. Some paleontologists think they will find hundreds of new dinosaurs if they keep looking.

Dinosaurs may have died because of fire and dust from volcanoes.

Dinosaurs Outside Your Window

Some small dinosaurs lived on after most other dinosaurs died. They learned to eat new plants. Their bodies became different so they could live on a cool Earth. Many years later, dinosaurs no longer looked the way they once did.

Paleontologists found out that birds may have once been dinosaurs. When you see a bird, try to think about how it is like a dinosaur. Paleontologists study fossils and bones from animals that lived at the time of the dinosaurs as well as animals that lived after the dinosaurs. Some of the bones and fossils paleontologists found look like birds.

The Archaeopteryx

The oldest bones paleontologists found that looked like a bird were from an animal called **Archaeopteryx**. The name *Archaeopteryx* means "ancient wing." Archaeopteryx lived at a time when there were many dinosaurs on Earth. It was about the size of the crows that can be seen today.

Archaeopteryx had teeth and a long tail like some dinosaurs and **reptiles**. Like a bird, Archaeopteryx had long legs and wings. Its feet had three claws that pointed forward and one claw that pointed backward.

Some dinosaurs changed when Earth changed. Scientists think they may have changed into the birds we see today.

Archaeopteryx also had three claws on each wing. It used those claws to catch the insects and small animals it ate. The claws could grip the branch of a tree.

The bones of Archaeopteryx were light like bird bones. Yet the big bone in its breast was flat. The same bone in a bird has a ridge. Paleontologists also saw that the skull was shaped like a dinosaur head.

Archaeopteryx had wings, feathers, and claws like birds today. It also had a tail like a dinosaur.

Paleontologists have also found marks in the rocks around the bones. These marks look like feathers. When Archaeopteryx died, its body fell into wet earth. More dirt covered the body. After millions of years, the dirt turned into rock. The body was gone, but the marks left in the earth by the feathers and the bones became a part of the rock.

Paleontologists are not sure if Archaeopteryx could fly even though it had wings and feathers. They think it may have been able to fly up into a tree and then glide down. The feathers just may have been a good way to keep warm. The feathers may also have been colored in a way to help this small dinosaur hide from big dinosaurs that would want to eat it.

Bird Bones in China

In a forest in China, paleontologists have found ancient bones that look like birds. These bones were found in rock that came from volcanoes. The rocks in China where the animal bones lay had clear marks that show the bodies were covered by feathers. The feet seem to have had webs like duck feet do.

The ancient dinosaur-bird bones found in China look like they came from a group of dinosaurs called **theropods**. Theropods walked on two legs. Tyrannosaurus rex was a theropod. Theropods that became birds were not as big as Tyrannosaurus rex. They were small like the size of a cat.

No one yet knows when the ancient dinosaur birds learned to fly. Short hops off the ground as the animals ran after their food may have led to flight. Finally, they did learn to fly. Little by little they became like the birds we see today.

Dino Notes

Some people wonder if any true dinosaurs could fly. There were reptiles that did fly, but they were not dinosaurs. All dinosaurs lived on land. No dinosaurs lived in the sea or flew in the air.

Fossils found in China show that this ancient animal had feathers.

Other Animals From Dinosaur Days

Some kinds of animals we see today once lived with the dinosaurs. Crocodiles, horseshoe crabs, and ants are some. The animals have changed little over millions of years.

There are other animals, like a kind of fish called a **coelacanth**, that scientists thought were long gone like the dinosaurs. Scientists had found bones and fossils from these animals in rocks from the time of the dinosaurs. Then someone found living animals. Scientists call all of these animals "living fossils."

An Ancient Fish

Fossils of coelacanths tell scientists that these fish were on Earth long before dinosaurs. Scientists thought that coelacanths had died with the dinosaurs.

In 1938, scientists found out they were wrong. Some people on a boat caught a strange fish in their net. The fish was blue and silver and about 5 feet long. The people did not know what kind of fish it was. They took it back to land to show people.

A scientist named J.L.B. Smith heard about the fish. He went to see it. Smith was very surprised by what he saw. He had seen coelacanth fossils, but here was a real coelacanth! It was as if J.L.B. Smith was looking at a living fossil.

Smith still had many questions. The fish had died, and the inside of it had been cleaned out. He had to study a whole fish. He and other scientists looked for many years. Finally, another coelacanth was caught 14 years later. Since then, groups of coelacanth have been found in other places in the ocean. They live near reefs and in sea caves. The coelacanth is not just a fossil. It is a living fossil!

Coelacanths were on Earth before the dinosaurs. They are still around today.

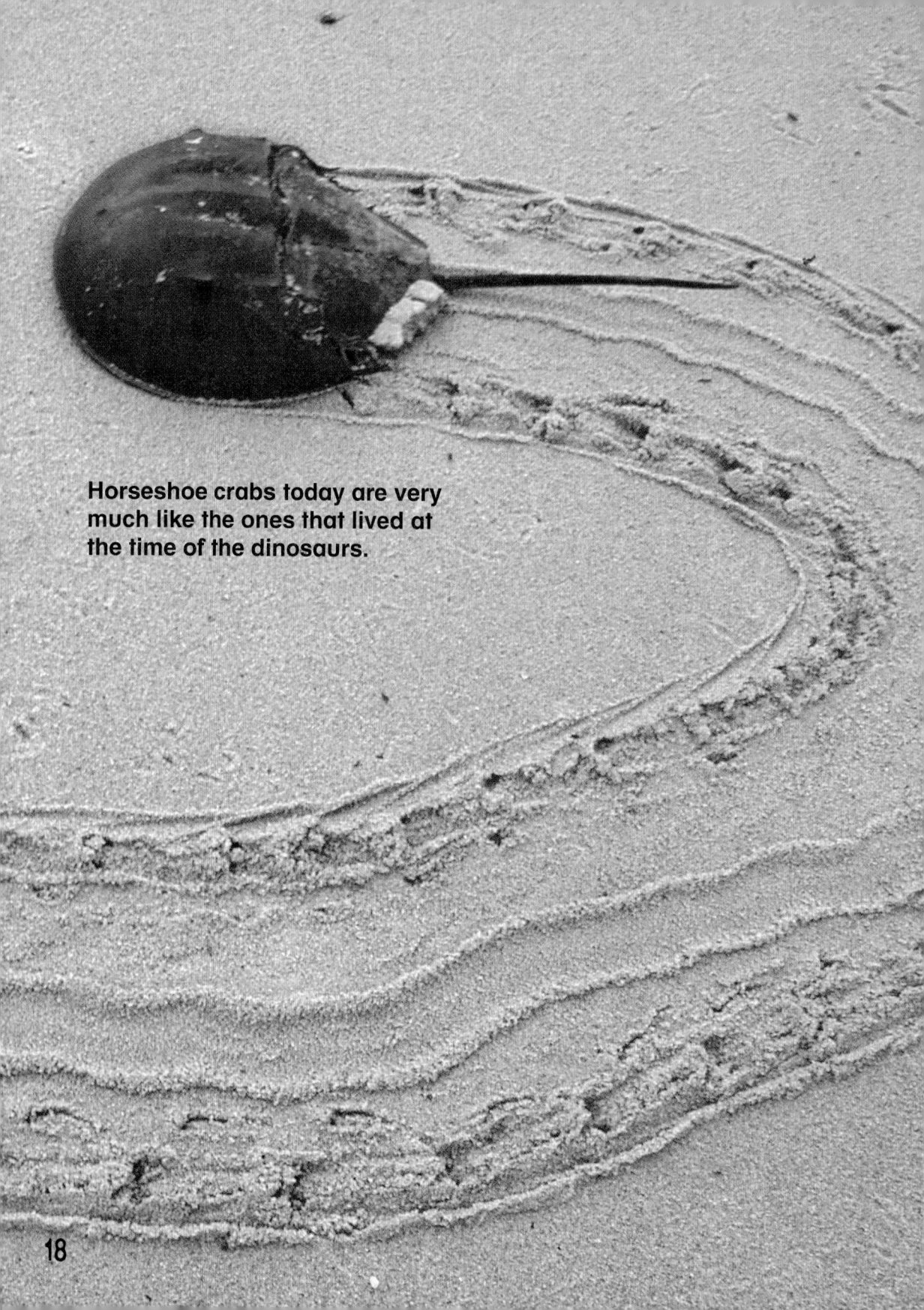

Horseshoe crabs today are very much like the ones that lived at the time of the dinosaurs.

The Horseshoe Crab

Some living fossils are animals that people see often today. These living fossils have been around for millions of years. Their bodies are just like the ancient fossils that scientists study.

One of these living fossils is the horseshoe crab. Its fossils date back to 100 million years before the dinosaurs. Many kinds of horseshoe crabs used to live on Earth. Now there are only four kinds.

Horseshoe crabs are not real crabs. Their mouth is more like a spider's mouth. They use five pairs of legs to walk with and one pair of short legs to eat with. True crabs have just five pairs of legs.

The horseshoe crab's body is covered by a hard shell. They also have a long tail that looks like a spike. They can grow to 2 feet long. Just as a snake sheds its skin, horseshoe crabs shed their shell many times as they grow.

Earth has gone through many changes during the time horseshoe crabs have lived. As the land broke apart and moved, the horseshoe crabs moved, too. As the seas cooled, the horseshoe crabs learned to live in cold water. As long as they could find food, they could live on Earth.

Long Live the Crocodile

Today's crocodiles are not as big or as small as the ancient crocodiles. However, their forms are much like the ancient crocodiles in many ways. One kind of ancient crocodile was as long as a bus. Like crocodiles today, it spent a lot of time in water and hid almost all but its eyes under the water. When a dinosaur walked by, the crocodile would jump out of the water and grab the animal. It also ate large fish.

Scientists think that crocodiles did not die with the dinosaurs. Crocodiles are hard to kill. They can swim in water that is not clean and eat bad food. They can even live a year with no food! If a crocodile is hurt, its body heals itself. Changes are no problem for these reptiles.

Insects in Amber

Many insects today were around at the time of the dinosaurs. Wasps and army ants have lived for a long time. They have not changed.

Insect fossils are not easy to find. An insect body is not hard like a bone. It does not last.

Crocodiles that lived at the time of the dinosaurs were much like today's crocodiles.

Scientists can find fossils of insects and spiders in amber.

Some of the best fossils are insects found in amber. Amber is tree **resin**. Insects that step in drops of the resin can stick there. The resin becomes hard and turns into amber. The whole body of an ancient ant caught in amber looks just like army ants today.

Living fossils can still be found in forests far away from people or deep in the ocean. These fossils show animals and insects that once lived with the dinosaurs. The world has changed, but they have not.

Dino Note

A piece of amber more than 100 million years old was found with a bit of spider web in it. Web fossils from spiders are rare.

Glossary

Archaeopteryx a dinosaur that looked like a reptile and a bird

coelacanth an ancient fish that scientists call a living fossil

crater a huge hole in the ground that may have been caused by a large rock that fell from space

meteors masses of stone or metal that fall to Earth from space

paleontologists scientists who study fossils and bones from the past, especially from the time of the dinosaurs

reptiles animals that have cold blood and lungs and are usually covered with scales

resin a sticky yellow or brown material that comes from some trees and later hardens

theropods dinosaurs that walked on two legs and ate meat

volcanoes places in the ground through which comes steam, ash, and flowing hot rock